THE HISTORY OF
BERLIN

D0521419

Imprint

Giebel, Wieland:
The History of Berlin
Second Edition – Berlin: Berlin Story Verlag 2012
ISBN 978-3-86368-029-9
Cover and typesetting: Norman Bösch
Translated from the German by E.F.S. Zbikowski

© Alles über Berlin GmbH
Unter den Linden 40, 10117 Berlin
Tel.: (030) 20 91 17 80
Fax: (030) 69 20 40 059
www.BerlinStory-Verlag.de
E-Mail: Service@AllesUeberBerlin.com

WWW.BERLINSTORY-VERLAG.DE

TABLE OF CONTENTS

< The Potsdamer Platz. We recommend this picture for the nostalgic. In those days the Platz was considered to be hectic. The location of the Potsdamer Strasse today can be recognized by the row of trees in the background.

Claudia Melisch, the director of the dig, shows Berlin Story and Historiale employees Berlin's oldest cemetery. Old St. Peter's church is incrusted in the photo.

NO TIME TO DRAW BREATH – HISTORY IS BEING MADE

No time to draw breath – History is being made. We barely have time to draw breath, but this was also true in the past. And there can be no question that history is being made in Berlin today. The twentieth century was shaped here, more or less, with the First World War, the Nazi period, the Second World War, the Cold War, the building of the Berlin Wall, and finally, its fall. When it fell on November 9, 1989, we just managed to get back into the mainstream of world history. Now, we Berliners feel that we have rejoined the ranks of the civilized peoples.

No time to draw breath – history is being made, as the post-punk band Fehlfarben sang in what was to become the hymn of the squats in the 1980s. History is being made, and occasionally forgotten as quickly as it is made. Like the Berlin Wall. Every tourist asks where it is, but nobody can sense the wall's awful horror any more, because practically nothing is left of it. You can see more from the imperial German period – the big prestigious buildings – and in the coming years the city castle will also be rebuilt. Yet the fall of the Berlin Wall is also affecting our understanding of our earliest history, when the city of Berlin was being founded. There is so much construction work going on today that the city's roots are being laid bare. First the archeologists do their job, and the developers' turn only

comes once they have finished. This sometimes gives rise to tension, because the archeologists want to excavate thoroughly, while the developers want to build as fast as they can. Nevertheless, mutual understanding is established in the course of time. Giving shape to the future on historic ground is quite a different matter from throwing up a car dealership or a furniture market on the outskirts of the city.

SINCE THE FALL OF THE BERLIN WALL, EXCAVATION OF THE PAST HAS PROCEEDED IN THE CITY'S MITTE BOROUGH.

Since 1989, Berlin's Mitte borough has been thoroughly revamped. The borough lay in East Berlin, behind the Berlin wall that ringed West Berlin, from the Western point of view. The prestigious government and company buildings, the big museums and theaters were always in Mitte. Today, both the government and, in the Reichstag building, the German parliament, are again in Mitte. And this was where Berlin started.

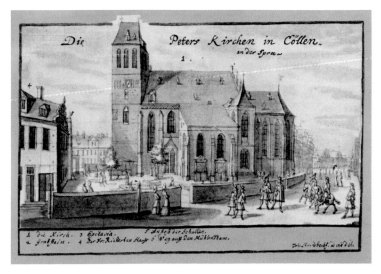

St. Peter's church as it originally appeared. This was where parish priest Symeon preached. He signed the first document in which the city is named. Stray dogs were sold in the market in the back.

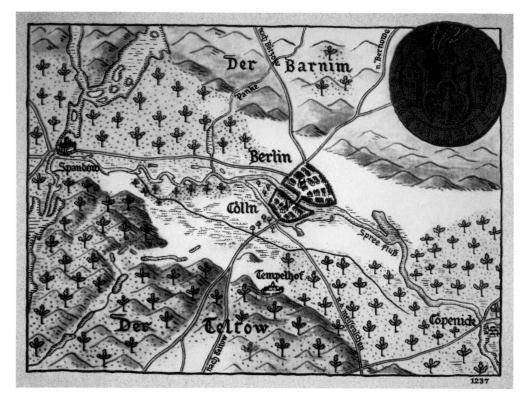

Berlin and Cölln in 1237, when they were first mentioned. The Spree flows lazily from Cöpenick in the South-east past Berlin to Spandau in the West. The thinly-settled valley had only been ice-free for 10,000 years.

The two founding spots can still be identified. Originally, Berlin was the Nikolai Quarter. Old Cölln, the other half of the twin city, was today's Fischer Island. Today it is occupied by high rises from the GDR period. The north of the island, between the two arms of the Spree River, is known today as Museum Island.

COMPARED WITH OTHER METROPOLISES, BERLIN IS A VERY YOUNG CITY.

Historic Cölln is the site of the most important excavations presently taking place. Round about the site where Saint Peter's Church once stood, the archeologists are studying a graveyard – in fact, several superimposed graveyards. Claudia Melisch, the director of the excavation, has also brought church foundations and a Latin school to light. The men and women of Berlin streamed to the excavations to get a glimpse of the city's early history.

Visitors from Athens, Rome, Istanbul and Cologne do not think that Berlin is all that old. The city is in fact a latecomer and a slow developer. When other cities already had ingenious sewer systems, democratic constitutions, amphitheaters and elegant baths, Berlin did not exist, even as a gleam in some visionary's eye. Here there were only swamps and wolves, fo-

Berlin comes from the German word for bear. S(igillum) secretum civitatis Berlin is written on the 1338 bear seal. Bears lived in the forests. But "berl-" could also come from an Old Polish/Slavic word for swamp.

The castle looks almost like a fortress around 1690. There are little shops beneath the arcades. The prestigious castle was first built in 1701. Today it is to be rebuilt.

xes, bears and wild boar, and a ford across the Spree. The inhospitable site, far from everything that was happening in the world, did not attract anyone. And how could it? There was nothing going on here. Although festivals, parties, trade fairs and big exhibitions take place here today, and Berlin and culture seem inseparable, this was not at all self-evident when the city was founded.

THE MOST AMERICAN OF ALL EUROPEAN CITIES.

Neither the happy and the successful nor the first-born children came to Berlin, because they preferred to stay home on their own farm or running their own business. Those who came to Berlin were those who were not going to inherit anything at home – no farm, no artisan's workshop, no property. This is what Berlin has in common with America and Australia. The people who left their homes were those who lacked elbow-room, were hungry, or were persecuted for social, political or religious reasons. This is one reason why it is appropriate to describe Berlin as the most American of all European cities. Roll up your sleeves and do something, build something. Love of liberty – initiative and passion – everybody gets his or her chance here.

HOHENZOLLERN.

The coat of arms of the Hohenzollerns -- they ruled Berlin for 500 years. In the beginning, the citizens angrily flooded the castle construction site. In the end they were proud of their Kaiser Wilhelm II.

The castle as seen from the Spree in around 1690. It went to ruin during the Thirty Years War (1618-1648). Berlin only had 6,000 inhabitants in 1648. Now things were finally improving again.

1237-1871 |
THE LONG AND WINDING ROAD TO CAPITAL CITY

At a ford on the Spree, on the trade route from the West to the East, a few people settled some time or other. Gradually, a settlement developed, a village, a very small city – nothing special. A market, a church, a school. Claudia Melisch found an oaken beam from a tree that was chopped down in 1192. That is how old – or young – Berlin is. The city's official date of birth is October 28, 1237: that is when the name "Cölln" is first mentioned in a document.

Two hundred years later, Duke Friedrich "Iron Tooth" laid claim to the middle part of the Spree Island to build a castle-like residence. Berlin had 8000 inhabitants who thought of themselves as free people; they did not want to be dominated. So it was that they resisted for eight years, submerging the construction site and chasing away the tax collectors. But Iron Tooth was tougher and got his residence. Berlin withdrew from the Hanseatic League of Free Cities.

Friedrich I, the baroque, spendthrift king of the days of absolute monarchy, with the insignia of power. He had the gigantic castle built, which is now to be rebuilt.

A royal coronation in Königsberg in 1701. A hand from heaven crowns the Prussian eagle. Friedrich I considered himself to be king by divine right. And he indeed crowned himself King in Prussia.

Two hundred years later, during the Thirty Years War, a Swedish army of 12,000 soldiers invaded. They plundered, burned and murdered. Dysentery and the plague continued the havoc. When the war ended in 1648, Berlin had a population of just 6,000. But from then on, the city prospered.

PROSPERITY THANKS TO HUGUENOTS FROM FRANCE AND TAXES ON BEER.

After the Thirty Years War, the Great Elector laid taxes on tobacco, coffee, tea, and above all beer. He had a wall built around Berlin so as to be able to collect customs duties. He brought in 17,000 French Huguenot religious refugees, had linden trees planted, and left his son Friedrich a thriving but highly fragmented and disunited country. Friedrich recognized the signs of the times, that is to say, that you counted for more if you had a kingdom and not "just" a margraviate. So he crowned himself in Königsberg in

Sophie Charlotte of Hannover was the second of Friedrich's three wives. She brought literature, music, the fine arts, and the philosopher Gottfried Wilhelm Leibniz to the small town of Berlin.

„Wenn man in der Welt was will dirigieren, es gewiß die Feder nicht macht, wenn es nicht mit completter Armee soutiniert (unterstützt) wird."

Friedrich Wilhelm I.

"long guys" – a regiment of taller-than-average soldiers. He enjoyed receiving them as a gift from friendly lords. Thanks to their height, they could load their muzzle-loading rifles faster, and in addition they could march at the same pace and drilled daily. At the end of his reign, the "money maker's" royal treasury was full. Berlin had a population of around 100,000, and every fourth inhabitant was a soldier.

FRIEDRICH THE GREAT – PHILOSOPHER, COMPOSER, COMMANDER-IN-CHIEF

1701. His subjects rejoiced, since they benefited from the new kingdom's glamour. The population of Berlin stood at 60,000 and the city was bankrupt because Friedrich I spent his money on ostentation and the construction of a new castle.

THE MONEY MAKER WITH A WEAKNESS FOR "LONG GUYS."

His son, Friedrich Wilhelm I, the soldier king, was thrifty, and choleric. His main hobby, in addition to his tobacco circle, whose members smoked and drank large amounts, was his "Potsdam giants" or

Friedrich suffered under his father's military discipline because, in contrast to the soldier king, he had a taste for the better things in life. He secretly learned French, read on the sly, and when he was caught,

Friedrich Wilhelm I with friends in the tobacco council. Politics were discussed -- foreign military men and diplomats were both invited to participate.

During his 27-year reign, Friedrich Wilhelm I paid off the colossal debts run up by his father, leaving his son with a full treasury.

Friedrich the Great playing the flute at a concert. He also composed music and took his musicians with him when he went to war. Playing the flute was a kind of therapy for him. As king, he had the Opera House on Unter den Linden built.

he had to look on as his father had the books thrown out. Friedrich wanted to run away with his friend Hans Hermann von Katte, but they were caught. On his father's orders, von Katte was beheaded before Friedrich's eyes.

When he mounted the throne in 1740, he abolished torture and censorship, championed freedom of the press, and had the first opera house built. Later he had St. Hedwig's Cathedral built for Silesian Catholics, as well as other buildings that are still standing on Unter den Linden. He gave the city international stature. Friedrich surrounded himself with European intellectuals and was, for example, a close friend of the French philosopher Voltaire.

LET EVERYONE BE HAPPY IN HIS OWN WAY.

Nevertheless, Friedrich's father had seriously misjudged him: Friedrich waged more wars, was victorious in twelve out of 15 big battles, and turned insignificant Prussia into a recognized European power.

Voltaire (left), the French philosopher whose ideas led to the French Revolution, was a close friend of King Friedrich II of Prussia for many years -- they are shown at Sanssouci in Potsdam.

Napoleon conquered Berlin on October 27, 1806, and stole the quadriga from the Brandenburg Gate. Berlin was occupied for two years and bled white. Queen Luise fled to Tilsit (today's Sovetsk). Prussia almost disappeared from the map.

Friedrich wanted enlightened, independent and thinking subjects who were not obliged to believe what their king believed. In addition to the buildings, we still enjoy his compositions – in wonderful recordings. Friedrich had no children and his nephew followed him on the throne. Friedrich Wilhelm II, on the contrary, had many children with his wife and his mistresses. He "spoke" with his ancestors at séances, promoted the arts, and had the Brandenburg Gate built in 1791. His eldest son, Friedrich Wilhelm III, was rather shy and had bourgeois tastes – but he married the most beautiful woman of his time, Luise, princess of Mecklenburg-Strelitz.

Alexanderplatz, named in honor of Tsar Alexander I during his visit to Berlin in 1805. Queen Luise (right) was smitten with Alexander and fought against Napoleon and the occupation of Prussia.

Alexander von Humboldt explored South America and worked for decades on the information he gathered. His main work is entitled "Kosmos." His brother Wilhelm founded the university, the forerunner of today's Humboldt University.

NAPOLEON'S SOLDIERS CONQUER BERLIN

Shortly afterwards, Napoleon annihilated the Prussian army, conquered almost all of Europe, and occupied Berlin in 1806. The self-crowned Emperor of the French bled the city white. Queen Luise opposed him and called for help from Russia's Tsar Alexander, with whom she got along well. At the same time she encouraged the Prussian reformers who modernized the army, educational system and system of government during the occupation.

Once the united European powers had beaten Napoleon in the Battle of the Nations at Leipzig in 1813, the new freedom of trade made economic and scientific development possible. Wilhelm von Humboldt had founded the University in 1810. His brother Alexander explored South America. Textile and metal-working factories were founded, and the architect Karl Friedrich Schinkel put a classical stamp on the city with Gendarmenmarkt square, the New Guardhouse, the Old Museum, the Friedrichswerder

The granite basin in front of the Old Museum in the Lustgarten, erected in 1834. Building inspector Christian Gottlieb Cantian (far left in the picture) had discovered the stone slab near Berlin. The work of art was ground and polished using newly-harnessed steam power.

Europe's and Berlin's citizens wanted a share of political power, and demanded freedom of thought and democracy. In March 1848 they fought beneath a black-red-gold flag on the barricades on Alexanderplatz.

Church, and the academy of architecture. From the latter, with just 30 colleagues, he managed all of the construction sites in Prussia. Berlin's population stood at over 248,000 inhabitants in 1830.

Economic power became the basis for a new self-consciousness which collided with the narrow, outdated rules that governed every aspect of life and stood in the way of progress. The real significance of the rising bourgeoisie found no political expression.

THE MARCH REVOLUTION FOR FREEDOM OF THOUGHT AND DEMOCRACY IN ALL EUROPE.

Everywhere in Europe, in Italy, Austria, Spain, and then in Paris, there were uprisings in 1848-49. At first it seemed as if the always-wavering king in Berlin would give in quickly. Friedrich Wilhelm IV

Friedrich Wilhelm IV did not understand his subjects. He was, after all, king by divine right. And anyway, he would rather have been an artist, an architect, a city planner.

The coffins of 183 victims of the March Revolution are displayed at the Gendarmenmarkt. Today's democracy did not fall from the sky, it had to be fought for. Many sacrificed their lives.

would rather have been an architect. He could spend the whole day drawing buildings and parks. He was overwhelmed by the uprising. Several times he ran in the night for his coach, so as to flee, but each time he returned. During a demonstration in front of the castle, shots were fired and two people died. Thousands built barricades and demanded the abrogation of censorship of the press and a national assembly, a German parliament. Germany did not yet exist as a united country. Hundreds died during the revolution, and 183 coffins were laid out at the Gendarmenmarkt. The king bowed down before the dead, first authorized a Prussian national assembly, and then dissolved it again. Everywhere in Europe, the uprisings were crushed. Nevertheless, their ideas and goals were realized later.

Bourgeois life on Unter den Linden around 1842. On the right the opera house, in the center the Königswache (Neue Wache) flanked by full-length statues of Generals Bülow and Scharnhorst (right).

August Borsig's machine factory and ironworks in Chausseestrasse. Between 1841 and 1847 187 locomotives were built and industrial products made. On the right, horses are pulling a locomotive.

INDUSTRIALIZATION AND REACTION

Industrialization on the one hand and restoration-minded rule on the other led to continually increasing tension. For example, the craft labor union was dissolved because it was suspected of being a front organization for democrats. Berlin continued, however, to grow as before, and more and more people moved to the city. In the 23 years between the 1848 March revolution and the founding of the German empire in 1871, the population doubled to 826,000 inhabitants.

James Hobrecht, who had studied at Schinkel's academy of architecture, was charged with planning an infrastructure to match the population growth. Now Berlin got a modern sewer system. A road network was developed and tenements were built to a standard plan: front building,

The first Prussian steamboat of 1817 had a 14 horsepower engine. Here the boat is on the Spree near Zelten (Haus der Kulturen der Welt). In the background Bellevue castle, today the residence of the German president.

Kaiser Wilhelm I leaves for the Franco-German war in 1870. He is on the left, sitting in the coach, but can barely be seen because artist Adolph Menzel preferred to depict the Berliners viewing the spectacle.

wings, and back building, in such a way that the newly-created professional fire department could always drive into the courtyard. The socially mixed tenements – expensive apartments in front and cheap ones in the back – were intended to prevent the development of London-style slums.

As far as education and university were concerned things were less rosy. But covered markets were built to architect Friedrich Hitzig's blueprints, and railroad king Bethel Henry Strousberg raked in the money and built a railroad empire. As always in Berlin, there were lots of parties. The theater boomed and was linked to gastronomy. In Julia Gräbert's theater on Weinbergsweg in the Prenzlauer Berg locality (in Pankow borough), 2000 ham sandwiches a day were sold to accompany wheat beer.

Unter den Linden around 1850. Gentlemen are clustered around the show window at E.H. Schröder's bookshop (opposite today's Berlin Story). On the left, customers wearing dress-coats and top hats are sitting in front of the Café Kranzler.

The proclamation of the German Empire in Versailles in 1871. Germany has won this time. Wilhelm I is not at all happy with his new role, but Bismarck (in white) has insisted on it.

1871-1918 | IMPERIAL BERLIN – THE CAPITAL CITY OF THE GERMAN EMPIRE

In 1806 Napoleon had occupied Berlin and demanded contributions which the city could scarcely make. Sixty-four years later, France allowed herself to be pro-

voked into a war. After losing the battle of Sedan however, France did not come to an honorable peace but rather fought on. After the annihilating defeat, she had to make exorbitant contributions – which for a short time allowed the German economy to blossom. But the mutual humiliation was to have consequences: After the First World War, the French took their revenge and bled Germany with the Versailles peace treaty. That led to the rise of Nazism.

The victorious troops return home in 1871 through the festively decorated Brandenburg Gate. France started the war, rejected a favorable peace offer after the Sedan battle, and paid heavily.

Unter den Linden around 1880. France's reparations payments favored Germany's rise. Technology, science and research throve in the long period of peace. Berlin was feeling good.

Franco-German friendship today is highly important within the European Union, so that such days may never return.

Bismarck founded the German empire, and not Wilhelm I, who would have preferred to remain King of Prussia instead of becoming emperor. His intuition – which was proved right – was that Prussia would become merged into Germany and would gradually lose its predominant position. Berlin, on the other hand, profited from its new role as imperial capital. Berlin grew into the biggest city between Paris and Moscow. It be-

came a powerful economic metropolis and drew large numbers of people, in particular many scientists, engineers, and also artists. A long period of peace and prosperity began for Berlin and for Germany as a whole.

Otto Lilienthal flying his glider in Berlin-Lichterfelde in 1895. He founded a machine factory at the age of 33, observed birds gliding for years and built his "wings" accordingly.

Reich chancellor Bismarck invited the European Powers to the Berlin congress in 1878 in order to carve up the Balkans and the Mediterranean. Diplomats from ten countries negotiated in Berlin for a month.

OTTO VON BISMARCK

The Social Democrats hated Bismarck and Bismarck hated them. They were not like him. The Social Democrats of the late 19th century were truly left-wing; class contradictions were sharpening. Bismarck stood at the center of the German empire for almost two decades: He created the empire and turned Berlin into a political metropolis. Nothing slipped past him, until he was disembarked by the new Kaiser, Wilhelm II, in 1890. The young monarch was the grandson of Wilhelm I. In between, Friedrich I, who died of cancer of the larynx, reigned for all of 99 days in 1888, the "year of the three Kaisers."

Bismarck settled down after his marriage in 1847, at the age of 32.

The first electric light shines on Potsdamer Platz in 1882 -- using technology developed by Siemens. After midnight, cheaper gas light was turned on. The first telephones were installed in Berlin in 1881.

The opening of the Reichstag in 1888 in the Berlin castle. Kaiser Wilhelm II assumes power -- and dismisses Bismarck (in white). At 29, Wilhelm II did not want a 73-year-old Reich president under his nose.

Before that, he mainly drew notice by going on drinking sprees, blowing his money, and sowing his wild oats in love affairs. He became bored as a trainee lawyer, interrupted his studies and traveled throughout Europe. He became familiar with all things human on his way to a political career. He was elected to the Prussian Landtag (parliament) in 1849 and attracted notice thanks to his oratorical talents. Wilhelm I named him premier in a crisis situation. Otto von Bismarck remai-

ned steadfastly loyal to the aged Kaiser's death in 1888.

The Social Democrats (SPD) were Bismarck's main domestic enemy. In or-

Children at the street pump in 1898. Berlin was the cleanest city in the world because Charité doctor Rudolf Virchow and architect James Hobrecht imposed the construction of a sewer system in the 1870s.

Dashing street sweepers take a break in the Lustgarten. Berlin's population shot from 493,000 in 1860 to 2,000,000 in 1908, quadrupling in fifty years.

der to limit the growth of the SPD, the Reich chancellor introduced medical and social insurance, and thus created the basis for the welfare state. He wanted to tie the workers to the imperial government.

KAISER WILHELM II PARTS WITH OTTO VON BISMARCK

Kaiser Wilhelm II, the grandson of Wilhelm I, fought his whole life long against his lame arm, a birth defect. His English mother Vicky, a daughter of Queen Victoria, wanted to mold him in the image of her father, Prince Albert. But Wilhelm was not a polished intellectual. Instead, he was practical-minded, open to technology, and enjoyed driving his Mercedes. He became Germany's first media star. Ever since, Germans have

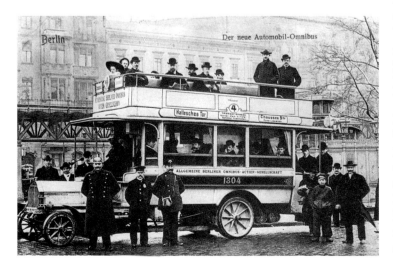

Berliners ride in Daimlers built in Berlin-Marienfelde. The first automobile omnibuses attracted crowds in 1905, ran on Friedrichstrasse, and were heated. Horse-drawn omnibuses had existed since 1846.

1914. Every New Year's Day, Kaiser Wilhelm II and his six sons marched with his generals (who are at a respectful distance) from the castle to the Neue Wache. He was the top media star of his time.

used the expression "Kaiser weather" for a beautiful sunshiny day, because it was only in such weather that the first movie cameras could be used – and it was the only weather in which the Kaiser appeared in public.

Historians debate the role played by Wilhelm II in the outbreak of the First World War. In 1914, the prevailing mood in many European countries was one of militarism. In each nation, the generals fed a feeling of confidence that the country could come out of a war victorious. Nobody could imagine that so many would die in battles of attrition. In the course of the First World War, Wilhelm II's political importance waned, and just before the armistice he and his heir, his eldest son abdicated. The former Kaiser spent the rest of his life relatively withdrawn, in exile in Holland. With that, the five-hundred-year rule of the Hohenzollern dynasty came to an end.

"Operator, how can I help you?" The telephone switchboard at number 70, Oranienburger Strasse around 1890. There were 28 multiple switchboards for 4411 (out of 10,000) customers. It was a new thing for women to be working here.

During the Spartakus uprising of 1919, machine gunners are stationed on top of the Brandenburg Gate. The German defeat led to an uprising staged by the Communist Party of Germany, which wanted to set up a soviet republic.

1918-1933 | BATTLEFIELD AND MODERN-DAY GOMORRAH – THE CAPITAL CITY OF THE WEIMAR REPUBLIC

At first, there was nothing golden about the "Golden Twenties" – the German expression for the "Roaring Twenties." And there was not much democracy, either. How were people, who had lived for 500 years in an authoritarian society, suddenly to become democrats? The Germans, most of them in any case, had entered the world war filled with confidence. But what they received was mainly news of deaths, and sometimes also coffins. Due to the British sea blockade, millions were starving, also in Berlin. In 1917, 300,000 workers struck in Berlin, and in early 1918 a half million German armaments workers went on strike. Their eyes were on Russia, where there had been a successful revolution that promised a fairer, happier future.

Children playing in a trench in Samariterstrasse in Friedrichshain in 1919. Kaiser Wilhelm had gone into exile in Holland. There was hard fighting especially in Berlin, but also in Bremen and Munich.

Fresh milk for Berlin. Every morning, Bolle company milk wagons rolled through the city. The needs of the population were met. "Bolle boys" enjoyed high regard.

The war ended in revolution. When defeat became obvious, the German sailors refused to allow themselves to be herded into a final battle against England. The revolution spilled over into Berlin within a few days. The SPD politician Philipp Scheidemann and the Spartacist leader Karl Liebknecht simultaneously proclaimed Germany a republic – the one, a democratic republic, the other a socialist republic. On January 15, 1919, socialists Liebknecht and Rosa Luxemburg were murdered by the paramilitary Freikorps soldiers who had suppressed the uprising.

The victors' reparations demands added up to 269 billion marks in gold ($32 billion), payable in installments through 1962. The flight of capital set in, the value of the currency fell, and French troops occupied the Ruhr because the installments were not paid on time. Hyperinflation wiped

This aerial view of Berlin dates from 1920. At the bottom of the picture, the Zeughaus (today the Deutsches Historisches Museum), opposite it the Lustgarten, to the right the city castle and to the left the museum island.

1926. The tempo of Berlin. Society became polarized. Rich and poor, people who were making it and those who were marginalized. Democracy was a new thing and was not yet working properly.

out livelihoods. In the Autumn of 1923, a loaf of bread cost billions in Berlin. The fear of losing one's livelihood, crime and the decay of social relations were the consequence.

Inflation was abruptly ended on November 15, 1923 with the introduction of the Rentenmark, a new, held covered currency. Customers filled the shops, and the boom lasted until the collapse of the New York Stock Market on Black Friday, October 24, 1929. These six years are called the "golden twenties."

It was only in 1920 that the Berlin that we know today came into existence. Seven cities (Charlottenburg, Schöneberg, Wilmersdorf, Neukölln, Spandau, Köpenick and Lichtenberg) and numerous other towns were incorporated, increasing the size of

There were never so many demonstrations in imperial days as in 1920s Berlin. The economic situation developed well only temporarily; it remained dependent on the world economy.

Stealing to satisfy need. Although some also pinched apples without being needy. Nobody really knows. The time of the great hunger came later, with the world economic collapse.

Berlin thirteen-fold. Greater Berlin now had 3.8 million inhabitants and represented the biggest industrial city on the continent. The secondary downtowns in the boroughs and the subcultures, the various local neighborhoods remained – often to this very day. With its 20 boroughs, the German capital city had a decentralized structure, different from Rome, Paris, Barcelona, Prague or London. The city was a world model for public mass transit; in 1928 the Berlin Transportation Company (BVG) was

The Berlin St. Bernard dog club on a promotional outing in 1928. The goal of the club is the "maintenance and strengthening of the race in its purity, nature, constitution, and perfectly finished appearance."

Josephine Baker first appeared on stage in Berlin in 1926 and drove men crazy. Many women, too. She was not allowed to appear in Prague, Budapest or Munich.

founded, which operated countless bus, street car, elevated railway, and subway lines. The driving force was the Social Democratic municipal transport councilor, Ernst Reuter.

SNORTING COCAINE, CELEBRATING AND PARTYING: THE GOLDEN TWENTIES

The revolution in Russia not only gave hope to the workers; it also dispersed Russia's aristocratic, bourgeois, intellectual and artistic elite. One hundred thousand Russians lived in Berlin in the 1920s, in fact more, since Berlin was also a way station to other destinations. Frenchmen, Hungarians, Czechs, Englishmen, Americans and East European Jews also came. The film industry boomed with "Metropolis" and "Nosferatu," movie theaters and dance halls throve. The exotic, the erotic, and everything curious, ecstatic and scandalous defined the city's image. The Comedian Harmonists, a close harmony ensemble, triumphed at the 3000-seat Plaza music hall, Otto Reutter, the singer, songwriter and comedian, and singer Claire Waldoff at the Wintergarten music hall. Josephine Baker appeared both with

Kurfürstendamm and its side streets were the center of the bohemian scene in the Roaring Twenties. The Größenwahn Café was home to artists, writers, and young ladies.

The title page of the program of the 1924 review "To all...! The big show in the big theater". Celebrating was the order of the day.

Programs that were somewhat attractive also played well in the rather bourgeois theaters.

The review "Take Your Clothes Off" was a success at the Komischer Oper. The naked flesh of both sexes and American swing music made life agreeable for those who could keep up.

and without her saxophone. In fact, she appeared (practically) without anything at all. It was a little bit as if strict parents had gone out, leaving the young people the run of the house.

Berlin had a good time in a hundred theaters. Everything modern and innovative moved to the city, and this was also the case with music. Vienna remained conservative, but Igor Stravinsky's piano concerts premiered at the Berlin Philharmonic, Alban Berg's

"Wozzeck" was performed, as was Bert Brecht's "Threepenny Opera" with music

The King of Afghanistan, Aman Ullah, came to visit Berlin in February 1928. Here Queen Turaya rides with justice minister Oskar Hergt in the Tiergarten. The Reichstag building is in the background.

The world economic crisis of 1929 ended the Roaring Twenties. Company bankruptcies, devaluation and mass unemployment favored the rise of Nazism.

by Kurt Weill. Just between 1927 and 1931, 41 new operas premiered in Berlin – Albert Einstein was thrilled.

In 1925, Berlin's population stood at four million. Not everyone was enthusiastic about the partying. As early as 1926, Adolf Hitler had named Joseph Goebbels gauleiter (Nazi district leader) of Berlin. It was clear to everyone that Germany's political gate would be decided in Berlin. Together with the Ruhr, Berlin was a communist stronghold. Goebbels and his brown-shirted SA storm troopers provoked pub brawls in the communist workers' quarters of Wedding, Moabit, Neukölln and Friedrichshain. At first, this was not expressed in election votes. In the 1928 Reichstag elections, the Nazi Party won 2.6 percent of the vote, and still only 5.8 percent in the municipal elections on November 17, 1929. The upturn for the Nazis began with the outbreak of the world economic crisis. The Social Democratic Party was squeezed on either

Even before the Nazi seizure of power, around 80,000 youths came to Potsdam in October 1932. It took seven hours for the long columns to march past Adolf Hitler.

Supporters of the Social Democrats demonstrate in the Lustgarten against the Nazi Party on May Day, 1932. The swastika on the flag has been crossed out with the symbol of the anti-Nazi "Iron Front" movement.

side by the Communist Party and the Nazis and lost its prominence. The Moscow-controlled communists fought the Social Democrats, and just four days before Hitler took power, its party newspaper "Rote Fahne" (Red Flag) berated them as "social fascists." The Communist Party tartly rejected an anti-Nazi alliance.

The press played an important role in the gradual increase in Nazi power. There was not yet any television, and radio did not yet exercise any mass influence. The press tycoons of the imperial age, Rudolf

Mosse and Leopold Ullstein, had entrusted their newspaper empires to their descendants. They were democratically minded, in contrast to the reactionary publisher Alfred Hugenberg.

The Nazi party became the strongest party in the Reichstag elections of July 31, 1932, garnering 37.3 percent of the vote. The Social Democrats obtained 21.6 percent and the Communists 14.3 percent. The Communists mainly fought against the Social Democrats.

Reichs chancellor Adolf Hitler celebrates the apparent continuity of the old (imperial) and new (Nazi) power with Reich president Paul von Hindenburg.

1933-1945 |
THE CAPITAL CITY OF THE THIRD REICH

How could it happen? Teachers like to ask their pupils this question. It all happened quite simply. The Nazis did not come to power through a putsch. People were aware of the dangers at the time. Newspapers, that is to say, public opinion, speculated about other solutions to the government crisis in early 1933. The "Frankfurter Zeitung" commented in its New Year's edition: "The powerful Nazi attack on democratic government has been warded off." Hitler's intention to take power was underestimated. On January 4, 1933, he met with former Reich chancellor Franz von Papen, who had governed for a few months with Reich president Paul von Hindenburg's emergency decrees. Von

The beginning of the ball season in 1934; young women get ready for an enjoyable evening. Life in no way came to a halt under Hitler, rather, for many Berliners it went on, apparently normally.

A Nazi torchlight parade to celebrate the naming of Hitler as Reichs chancellor on January 30, 1933. This photo was taken at a reconstitution in June 1933 because the original photo was less impressive.

Papen's government had ultimately collapsed. Von Hindenburg was old and lethargic. The banker in whose house Hitler and von Papen met said in 1947: "The common effort made by businessmen and financiers was aimed at seeing a strong leader come to power in Germany, a man who would form a government that would remain in power for a long time ... A common interest of the economy consisted in fear of Bolshevism and the hope that the Nazis – once they were in power – would set up an enduring political and economic foundation." Von Papen persuaded the old Reich president to name the Nazi boss Reich chancellor. He saw Hitler as a puppet: "In two months we shall have so squeezed Hitler into a corner that he will squeak!" But Hitler only played the milquetoast at the beginning.

Nudism. Forbidden at first, nudism gradually won favor in the Third Reich. The "Union for Bodily Improvement" was devoted to "the racial, health and moral improvement of the people's strength."

The Reichstag fire in the night of February 28, 1933. On the following evening the "Order of the Reich president for the protection of the people and the government" (The Reichstag Decree) was promulgated. It made possible the repression of all of the opponents of the Nazis. Basic rights were abolished and Hitler ontained full dictatorial powers. To this day, there is debate as to who set the fire. The Dutch communist Marinus van der Lubbe was arrested in the burning Reichstag building and sentence to death.

from the beginning they showed where their path led.

The Reichstag building burned on the evening of February 27, 1933. There is much evidence that the arsonist was a deranged Dutchman, acting alone. Historians have written many books on the question. The arson attack came just at the right moment for the Nazis. They got the Reich president to sign the "order for the protection of the people and the government," better known as the Reichstag fire decree. Von Papen backed the measure and thereby dest-

Once they had gained power, the Nazis used every opportunity to expand their position, so that Hitler could occupy a quasi-dictatorial position. And right

The Nazi boycott action against Jewish shops on April 1, 1933. The anti-Jewish propaganda was especially aimed at foreign countries, which is why the Nazis used English-language posters.

May 10, 1933. At the Opernplatz (today's Bebelplatz with the inset memorial) the Nazi German Student Union burns books that are considered to "go against the German spirit."

royed his own position of power. For this decree "for defense against communist acts of violence that endanger the state" gave Hitler almost unlimited authority. In the following days, the country's legal foundations were tailored to Hitler's taste and the course of justice perverted. The "Enabling Act" of March 23, 1933 allowed the government to enact laws without the approval of parliament or the Reich president. All this happened within a few weeks. By June, 1933, all parties except for the NSDAP (Nazi Party) were outlawed, and "Führer orders" had the force of law. Thus the Nazis created an apparently legal basis for their power.

They used the Reichstag fire as a pretext to clear their opponents out of their way, initially above all the communists and left intellectuals who engaged in resistance. People

Hitler gives a speech at the Lustgarten on May Day, 1935. The original photo caption reads: "Hitler youths sit high up on the iron railing of a window in the Berlin castle in order to catch a glimpse of the Führer."

February 18, 1943. "Do you want total war?" Following the Stalingrad defeat, Reich propaganda minister Joseph Goebbels was trying to reestablish unshakeable determination to win the war.

were put in concentration camps (not extermination camps) on the basis of lists that had been drawn up before January, 1933.

The persecution of the Jews began immediately. The storm troopers of the SA attacked shopowners, looted shops, and destroyed the offices of Jewish doctors and lawyers. East European Jews in the Scheunen quarter in the Mitte borough were bullied and tormented. "Jewish" department stores and hotels were attacked, and their customers and guests put under pressure. On April 1, 1933, Nazis stood in front of Jewish-owned shops everywhere in Germany and called for a boycott. They included the KaDeWe, Hertie, and Woolworth's department stores.

On May 10, 1933, an action led by the German Student Association culminated in the book burning at Opernplatz. Their

"justification" stated that "the Jewish spirit, which has revealed itself in the total

Claus Schenk, Count von Stauffenberg knows that many Germans will reject his attempt to assassinate Hitler. Nevertheless, he did not want to become "a traitor to his own conscience."

Otto Weidt is a staunch opponent of the Nazis. He runs a broom- and brush-making shop. The majority of his employees are blind Jews. He protected them with bribery and fake passports.

wantonness of its world agitation, and which has already formed a deposit in German literature, must be expunged therefrom."

Under Hitler the number of unemployed fell from six million in 1932 to 1.6 million in 1936 – but the cause was not an economic miracle, rather, it was the debt-financed arms build-up. Agriculture in contrast was depressed. The propaganda slogans against the Jews disappeared during the 1936 Olympic Games because Germany was to be presented as friendly and open to the world.

THE ANNIHILATION OF THE EUROPEAN JEWS

The "final solution of the Jewish question" was one of the main goals of Nazi policy. On January 20, 1942, at the Wannsee Conference, in a villa in a Berlin suburb, they discussed the practical realization of

Several thousand concentration camps and six extermination camps were used to murder millions of people. Six million Jews were murdered by the Nazis between 1933 and 1945.

A wasteland of ruins. The war that was started in Berlin comes back home. 68,000 tons of bombs fell on Berlin. An air raid involved up to a thousand airplanes.

the deportation of all European Jews for annihilation in the East. Six million Jews were systematically and even industrially murdered – a unique crime in world history. But three million Soviet prisoners of war, three million Polish Catholics and two million East European slave laborers were also murdered. Social Democrats, opponents, homosexuals, Sinti and Roma were also killed.

Around 173,000 Jews lived in Berlin in 1933. Two-thirds of them managed to emigrate, most of them escaping with their bare lives. But 55,000 Jewish Berliners were murdered, and only 9,000 survived in the underground or thanks to marriage to a non-Jewish partner. From September 1941, they had to wear the yellow star of David, and in the following year they were denied meat, milk and wheat, and had to

Camouflage nets are stretched over Charlottenburger Chaussee (today's Straße des 17. Juni) before the Brandenburg Gate in 1941. The intention was to mislead Allied aerial reconnaissance.

Hitler also sent children to war. For their last assignment they get weapons training and are sent to the front. Thousands of them die in the futile defensive battle around Berlin.

turn in woolen and fur clothing. Many "Aryan" Berliners hastened to grab Jewish property, taking over professional businesses, shops, department stores and hotels. After 1945 it was difficult to prove these cases of injustice. Few acted justly. One of the few was Otto Weidt, who ran a workshop for the blind which the German army considered necessary for the war effort. This allowed Weidt to save blind Jews. There was resistance on the part of Communists, Social Democrats, and Jews; from churches, trade unions, the occupied countries, and from more and more ordinary, decent people. Resistance within the military acted for the most part in Berlin. The attempted July 20, 1944 assassins grouped around Claus Count von Stauffenberg met regularly in Berlin.

Bombed out. Alexandrinenstraße and Oranienstraße in Kreuzberg after February 3, 1945, when 1,000 American B-17 bombers attacked in two waves with high explosive and incendiary bombs.

The destroyed Reichstag building on May 2, 1945. Yevgeny Khaldei, the Russian photographer, encrusted the aircraft and the tanks in the photo. Hitler committed suicide in the Führerbunker on April 30, 1945.

THE WAR COMES HOME TO BERLIN

The first air attacks against the capital of the Reich took place in 1940. But initially

the Royal Air Force (RAF) did not have many aircraft. That changed with the air battle over Berlin, with 19 large-scale attacks between November 1943 and March 1944. More than 800,000 Berliners were made homeless, and 7,400 died. Older Berliners can still remember the routine: Preliminary alarm. Prayers. Air raid shelter. High explosive bombs, blockbusters. Incendiary bombs. All clear, and the hope not to have joined the ranks of the bombed-out.

In April 1945 the environs of Berlin became a battlefield. A million soldiers, including many 14- to 16-year-old children, and old men, were sent to the Oderbruch lowlands 50 miles east of Berlin, where they were to stop 2.5 million Soviet soldiers, 6,000 tanks and 7,500 aircraft. It was all over in two weeks. The totally ruined Reich capital capitulated on May 2, 1945. The final battle probably cost

The sign in the background reads: "Men between the ages of 16 and 70 belong in action, not in the bunker." Propaganda with anti-tank Panzerfäuste for the last assignment. 175,000 members of the Volkssturm militia died.

At war's end: No trees are left standing in the Tiergarten. They were cut down for firewood. Cabbage was planted on the cleared ground. The food situation was dramatic.

250,000 lives, including those of at least 80,000 Soviet and 100,000 German soldiers; the remainder were civilians.

In the Führer's bunker in Wilhelmstraße, whose location is today indicated by a marker, Adolf Hitler and his spouse Eva Braun, together with Reich propaganda minister Joseph Goebbels ("Do you want total war?") hoped for a miracle. Madga Goebbels poisoned her six children. Hitler complained of the SS soldiers and secretaries who were drunkenly celebrating the destruction of their world. Hitler shot himself and his followers burned his body at the bunker entrance. Six days after the capitulation of Berlin, the German armed forces surrendered unconditionally in Karlshorst, in the Berlin borough of Lichtenberg.

Armed with automatic weapons, Soviet soldiers, hardly more than children, storm the Frankfurter Allee subway station in Friedrichshain (then the Horst Wessel borough) on the arterial road to Frankfurt on the Oder.

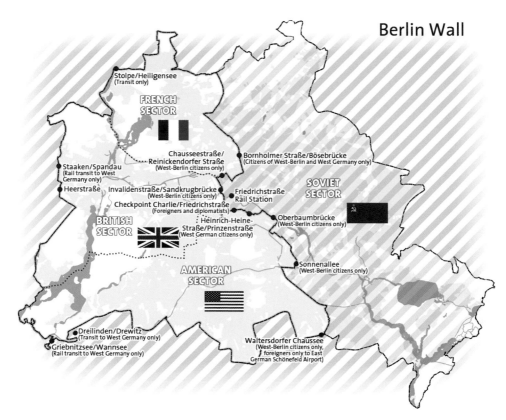

Berlin Wall

Stolpe/Heiligensee
(Transit only)

FRENCH SECTOR

Chausseestraße/
Reinickendorfer Straße
(West-Berlin citizens only)

Bornholmer Straße/Bösebrücke
(Citizens of West-Berlin and West Germany only)

Staaken/Spandau
(Rail transit to West
Germany only)

Heerstraße

Invalidenstraße/Sandkrugbrücke
(West-Berlin citizens only)

Friedrichstraße
Rail Station

Checkpoint Charlie/Friedrichstraße
(Foreigners and diplomatists)

SOVIET SECTOR

Oberbaumbrücke
(West-Berlin citizens only)

Heinrich-Heine-
Straße/Prinzenstraße
(West German citizens only)

BRITISH SECTOR

Sonnenallee
(West-Berlin citizens only)

AMERICAN SECTOR

Dreilinden/Drewitz
(Transit to West Germany only)

Griebnitzsee/Wannsee
(Rail transit to West Germany only)

Waltersdorfer Chaussee
(West-Berlin citizens only,
foreigners only to East
German Schönefeld Airport)

In 1945, Berlin was divided into four sectors for the USA, Great Britain, France and the Soviet Union. The wall around West Berlin was built in 1961 because three million people had fled the GDR.

1945-1989 | THE HOTTEST FRONT IN THE COLD WAR – THE DIVIDED CITY

"You see them poking about in the ruins, broken, numb and shivering; hungry human beings without any will, any purpose or goal in life, reduced to such animal functions as the search for food and shelter to try and stay alive until the following day." Those are the words that U.S. war correspondent William L. Shirer wrote in

Berlin

West Berlin was a front line city in the Cold War, an island in the middle of the GDR, linked to the West by three aerial corridors.

Unter den Linden in 1945. Cows graze in the courtyard of the Humboldt University. In the background, the State Opera building.

May 2, 1945. Yevgeny Khaldei's photo has become an icon of pictorial history. It represents the end of the Second World War in our collective consciousness. The photo, titled "the banner of victory," was immediately published in Moscow.

the first days after the end of the war. Berlin had become the biggest pile of ruins in Europe. In the eleven weeks preceding the end, 200,000 people had fled. Of 4.3 million Berliners, 2.7 million remained, two-thirds of them women, most of the remainder children. In the days before and after the capitulation, Red Army soldiers raped innumerable women in Berlin.

"It is amazing how fast life has reasserted itself. People are clearing the heaps of rubble, in

Friedenau (in the Tempelhof-Schöneberg borough) they have water again," Marget Boveri wrote in her diary on May 13, 1945.

1945. The Lutter & Wegner wine tavern at the Gendarmenmarkt in Charlottenstraße. Today the restaurant looks a little different. You have to party – that runs through every period of Berlin's history.

A C-54 lands at Tempelhof airport. The Soviet occupation power closed the roads to West Berlin. The 278,000 flights of the Berlin airlift provided food for 2.2 million people over a period of 15 months.

BLOCKADE AND AIRLIFT

Lucky Strike and Pall Mall cigarettes were the most widely accepted currency on the thriving black market. Barter was practically the only form of commerce in the icy winters of 1946-47 and 1947-48. It was only on Monday, June 21, 1948, that the Deutsche Mark was introduced, first in the West German occupation zones and then in West Berlin. Thereupon, the Soviets closed all access roads to West Berlin. General Lucius D. Clay, the U.S. military governor, did not shilly-shally: within a few days he organized the Operation Vittles airlift to provide West Berlin with food and coal. Products "made in blockaded Berlin" were flown out. Lieutenant Gail Halvorsen was the first pilot to throw chocolates and chewing gum from his "candy bomber."

On the day of currency reform, the old hundred Mark bills became worthless and the D-Mark was introduced in West Germany. The currency reform was the excuse for the Berlin blockade.

On June 17, 1951, Soviet troops smash the first uprising in the Eastern bloc. At Leipziger Platz demonstrators stone tanks. The democratic West is doing well economically.

THE JUNE 17, 1953 UPRISING IN EAST BERLIN

It was the first of many uprisings in Eastern Europe. Poland followed in 1956, Prague in 1968. Each time, Soviet tanks rolled into the "worker- and peasant-states," each time there were deaths, and each time "Western secret agents" were blamed.

The year before, in July 1952, the East German Socialist Unity Party (SED) had decided to "build socialism at a forced pace." More work was to be done without an increase in pay. The supply situation in the German Democratic Republic (GDR) was catastrophic; there was less to eat than during the war. The prosperity gap with the West grew. In 1952, 180,000 people escaped to the West, 331,000 in 1953. The GDR had to pay high reparations to the USSR, and spent a lot on armaments and heavy industry. The strikes began on the construction sites in Stalinallee.

Demonstrators from the East march through the Brandenburg Gate to the West. Since then, the road's name has been Straße des 17. Juni. Walter Ulbricht, the strong man in the SED and the GDR, was Stalin's proconsul.

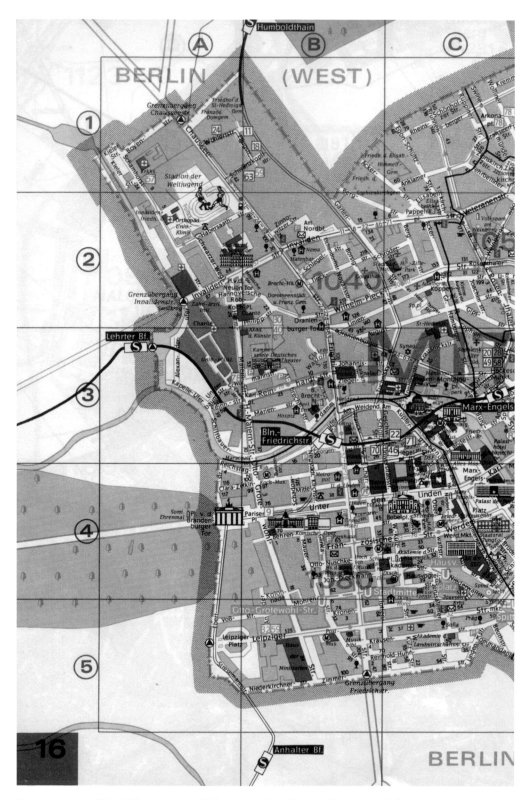

Terra incognita. The 1980 city map published by the East German Tourist Publishing Co. ends at the wall. The subway lines are not shown. City maps published in West Berlin always showed the whole city.

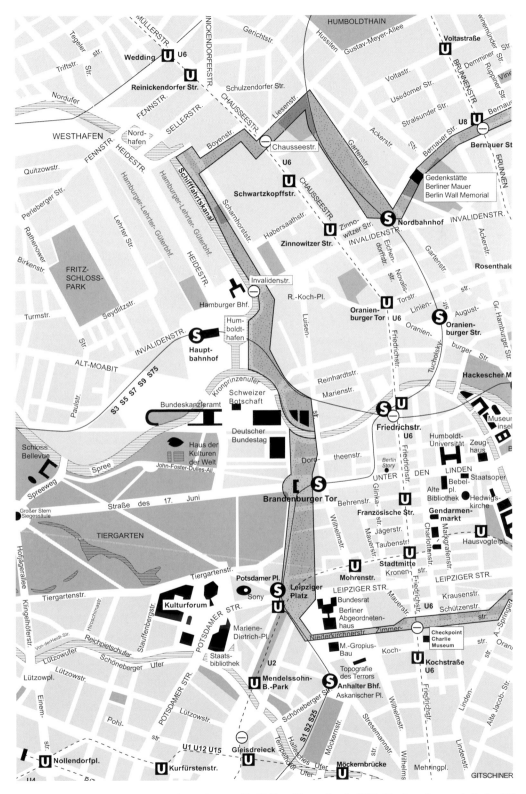

The Berlin Wall divided the city from August 13, 1961 to November 9, 1989. During that period, the U6 subway line traveled past "ghost stations" in East Berlin. The West had been walled in.

Peoples Policeman Conrad Schumann, age 19, leaps into the West. Peter Leibing photographed the scene, which was also filmed. The first barbed wire has been laid along Bernauer Straße.

AUGUST 13, 1961,
THE BUILDING OF THE BERLIN WALL

The GDR could not convince its own citizens of the superiority of socialism. Precisely the young people, who were to be won to the new system, felt they had no future in the country. Half of the refugees were under 25. Between the founding of the GDR in 1949 and the building of the Berlin Wall in 1961, one East German in six left the country – in particular the young, the bright, and the social climbers.

The construction of the Berlin Wall on a Sunday morning came as a surprise. The West Berlin politicians suspected nothing. Harrowing scenes took place. Some 50,000 East Berliners could no longer go to their jobs in West Berlin. Fears of a third world war hung heavy in the air. And the scars of the

Families were torn apart. The Berlin Wall divided the city for 28 years. The border between East and West Germany was closed for 37 years. Hundreds died attempting to reach freedom in the West.

Confrontation at Checkpoint Charlie on October 27, 1961. Soviet tanks roll up in the Mitte borough (in the background). American tanks in Kreuzberg borough rush to meet them.

Second World War had not yet healed; Berlin had not yet been rebuilt.

A quarter of a million West Berliners demanded that the USA do something, but it respected the Soviet zone of influence. Vice President Lyndon B. Johnson came together with Lucius D. Clay, who had realized the Berlin airlift. Clay became a rock of refuge for West Berliners, and a guarantee of freedom as John F. Kennedy's personal representative in Berlin (Sept. 1961-May 1962).

FOUR GENERATIONS OF THE BERLIN WALL

It took a decade and a half for the GDR to go from concertina wire to a 12-foot high

West Berlin policemen standing in West Berlin at the Brandenburg Gate on October 31, 1961. British soldiers put up the concertina wire to prevent rash protest actions on the part of West Berliners from breaking out.

A family flees through a ground floor window across Bernauer Straße on August 17, 1961. The apartment building is in East Berlin, the sidewalk in West Berlin. Many succeeded in escaping in the first days.

wall of pre-formed L-shaped concrete modules. The Berlin Senate's city planners describe the wall in these terms: "The Berlin Wall was a large construction work. It was a complex, continually-changing barrier that was always becoming more impenetrable. It was composed of a broad death strip with numerous blocking and surveillance systems. In exposed places like the Potsdamer Platz, the generally 75-yard wide border strip was extended to up to 550 yards. The projected "border security facility 90" was to be equipped with sensors, infrared gates, vibration and signal detectors and automatic searchlights. But the GDR

The Potsdamer Platz in November, 1975. The wall is almost twelve feet high. Behind it in East Berlin are a death strip, tank obstacles and fences. In the background stand the ruins of the "Haus Vaterland" building, once a temple of amusement.

John F. Kennedy visits Berlin on June 26, 1963. Willy Brandt, the mayor of Berlin, stands next to him, together with German chancellor Konrad Adenauer. One million Berliners line the streets.

collapsed before this "high tech border" could be realized."

out of Berlin with ultimatums and bullying.

"ICH BIN EIN BERLINER"

The division of the city seemed to be sealed in concrete when John F. Kennedy came for the 15th anniversary of the Berlin blockade in 1963. But then a million Berliners gathered in the square in front of the Schöneberger town hall heard his words: "All free men, wherever they may live, are citizens of Berlin, and, therefore, as a free man, I take pride in the words 'Ich bin ein Berliner'!" A barrier had been set to Soviet greed. Before 1963, Nikita Khrushchev had tried several times to drive the Western Powers

Berlin celebrates "Ich bin ein Berliner" – the speech given from the balcony of the Schöneberg town hall. Some Berliners think that Kennedy arrived too late – two years after the building of the Berlin Wall.

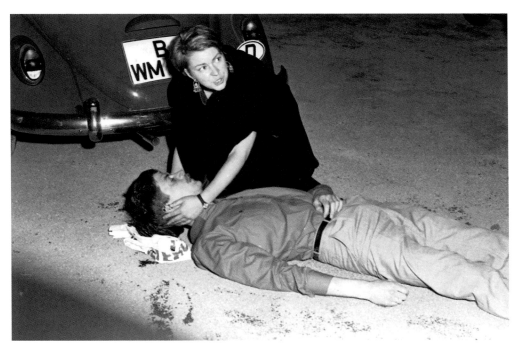

Student Benno Ohnesorg was shot on June 2, 1967 by policeman Karl-Heinz Kurras in the course of a demonstration against the Shah of Iran. Kurras was a Stasi spy. That was first discovered in 2009.

THE 1968 STUDENT MOVEMENT

Just four years later, a completely new age had begun. Many West Berlin students were criticizing the U.S. war in Vietnam

and denouncing the totalitarian systems in Spain, Portugal, Greece and Turkey. They believed that state of emergency measures might be used to suppress the opposition in the Federal Republic of Germany. They saw a danger in Axel Springer and his "Bild" newspaper company.

Older people and many politicians, on the other hand, were reminded of the disturbances of the Weimar Republic. They wanted a peaceful system and were satisfied with both the economic boom and the state of democracy. Two apparently irreconcilable ideologies were apparently at loggerheads.

On June 2, 1967, a policeman in Berlin shot dead

A pro-America rally at the town hall in Schöneberg. Many Berliners and the BILD newspaper remember the airlift, the Berlin Wall and Kennedy. Social contradictions are resolved in militant confrontations and disturbances.

Student leader Rudi Dutschke attempts to storm the courthouse on November 27, 1967, at the beginning of the trial of Kommune I co-founder Fritz Teufel. Dutschke was shot in the head five months later.

Benno Ohnesorg, one of the students protesting the oppression of the Iranian people. Meanwhile the Shah of Iran was enjoying Mozart's "The Magic Flute." The policeman, Karl-Heinz Kurras, was a spy on the payroll of the East Berlin state security services. This was only revealed in 2009, long after the fall of the Berlin Wall and Kurras' own retirement.

The student movement only took place in the West. The rioting went on for over a year. A small terrorist splinter group was then formed, the "Red Army Fraction." Far more student acti-vists became hippies, while others began the long march through the institutions, becoming teachers, professors – or, in the case of Joschka Fischer, foreign minister.

Following the attempted assassination of Rudi Dutschke by a right-wing extremist on April 11, 1968, demonstrators set fire to Springer company vehicles. The publisher was accused of conducting a hate campaign.

August 12, 1951. The World Festival of Youth and Students in East Berlin. Stalin in the Lustgarten in front of the cathedral. The socialist countries and socialist organizations in the West sent 26,000 participants.

At the same time critics of the East German regime were being kidnapped in West Berlin. The GDR wanted to strengthen its image abroad. The demonstrations attracted less and less attention in the West in the following years.

Can a society be built with enthusiasm, ardor, joyful creativity and the hope for a just, equal and peaceful life? Various versions of this vision have miscarried in the GDR, Cuba, Russia, and China. Personal hopes and dreams apparently have pride of place over heteronomous, imposed and collective visions of society.

The GDR suffered from its Stalinist socialism, imported from the Soviet Union. It was not the people who had fought for a new type of society at the end of the Second World War, rather the unloved occupation power decided on the new rules. The Soviets were unloved not only because of the rapes immediately after the war, but also because the GDR was financially bled white while the U.S. coddled up West Germany.

The GDR party leadership had been stationed in Moscow during the Second World War. They were flown to Germany on April 30, 1945 and immediately began to institute a dictatorship on the Soviet model.

960. The fairy tale fountain in Friedrichshain Volkspark. The fountain was restored and maintained in the GDR, even though it dates from the imperial period (ordered in 1896, finished in 1913).

Stalinallee. "Workers palaces" are built for the laboring classes where the battle for Berlin once raged (see page 41, bottom photo). The June 17, 1953 uprising began on these construction sites (see page 45).

The other Germans, in the West, could travel to Italy on vacation, as Johann Wolfgang von Goethe once had done; they had modern domestic appliances, smart cars, and a thriving consumer society. The people living in gray, inefficient socialism on the other hand needed a lot of persuasion to believe in the superiority of their system. In addition, it was precisely the young, well-trained and able-bodied citizens who had fled. Those who remained were often the sluggards and those who did not want to abandon their family.

1968. The television tower at Alexanderplatz is being built, an engineering marvel. Walter Ulbricht, the boss of the SED, wants it exactly here, and not in the Friedrichshain Volkspark.

GDR workplace combat groups march on May Day 1983 to Alexanderplatz. Most members of the paramilitary units were also members of the SED.

THE 1980S IN THE EAST AND IN THE WEST

Two decades after the construction of the Berlin Wall, people in both the East and the West had got used to the situation. The two societies were drifting apart.

Only pensioners came to the West for a visit. Fewer food packages were being sent to the East because there were enough of the basic necessities in the GDR. Opportunism was spreading under the SED dictatorship. Society marched in lock-step. Privately, you could say bad things about the society, and as in all authoritarian, dictatorial systems, jokes acted as lightning rods for discontent. Real opposition, on the other hand, existed practically only beneath the umbrella of the Lutheran church.

The desire for reunification had also evaporated in

The Reichstag building without its cupola, with a soccer field for the people. The words "for the German people" are engraved on the building. Several teams could play here simultaneously in the 1970s, 1980s and 1990s.

President Ronald Reagan speaks at the Brandenburg Gate on June 12, 1987. "Mr. Gorbachev, open this gate. Mr. Gorbachev, tear down this wall." It was to take just two more years.

West Berlin. The West Berlin economy was subsidized by the Federal Republic of Germany. Anyone who wanted to avoid military service could go to West Berlin. It was a shining island in the middle of socialism. The Berlin Wall had become a part of everyday life, it had ceased to inspire horror.

But this picture was not completely accurate. A few Germans remained dedicated to unity – and were reviled as revanchists. Nor did Ronald Reagan and many other Americans want to come to terms either with the division of the country or with socialism in the world. When the first signs of political opening became visible in the Soviet Union, and when the GDR came grinding to a halt with decaying cities and a decaying economy, opposition forces began to make themselves heard.

October 21, 1989. Günter Schabowski, a member of the politburo and boss of the Berlin district leadership for the SED, speaks to demonstrators. That had never happened before. The SED's power is already wavering considerably.

Hundreds of thousands of people gathered on Alexanderplatz on November 4, 1989. It was the biggest independent demonstration in the history of the GDR. It was organized by the people, not by the Party.

THE FALL OF THE BERLIN WALL IN 1989

The rulers could no longer rule in the old way, and the masses no longer wanted to live in the old way. So it came to revolution, to the Peaceful Revolution. Once Gorbachev with his concept of reform had come to power in the Soviet Union, the aged rulers in the GDR no longer had "a big brother" – or any ideas of their own, as to how to proceed. They borrowed billions from West Germany. The state security service (Stasi) was also of no help. Listening in on all conversations and knowing everything does not provide one with a prospect for the future. Astoundingly: In 1989 the state security ministry had 90,000 full-time employees and 180,000 part-timers on the payroll. That summer Hungary opened its borders with Austria. Thousands

Checkpoint Charlie on November 9, 1989, after 11:14 p.m. Günter Schabowski had earlier announced on television with regard to travel rules: "To the best of my knowledge, this becomes ... this is immediate, without delay."

November 10, 1989. Italian journalist Maria Luisa Cocozza reports live on the fall of the Berlin Wall. Germans embrace one another with tears in their eyes.

went on holiday and were never seen again in the GDR – they left everything behind. Others clambered over the walls of the FRG embassy in Prague.

Now the opposition began to get organized in the GDR. At first, there were only a few hundred human rights activists, upstanding people, but nothing like a mass movement. As criticizing the socialist system was still dangerous.

An independent mass demonstration in the Square of Heavenly Peace in China had been gunned down in June 1989. This experience hung continually over events in Berlin. Would the SED government shoot the people again? The old party leadership had been forced to retire after the 40th anniversary of the GDR in October 1989, but the new leadership was not firmly in the driver's seat. The system was to be kept alive with reforms, in particular freedom to travel.

Totally unexpectedly, the new spokesman for the Politburo, Günter Schabowski,

announced on November 9, 1989, that the people could travel to the West "beginning immediately." This misunderstanding was shown again and again on Western television. Unheard-of scenes took place at the border crossing points between East and West Berlin. The people crowded against the gates until they were opened. The old gentlemen of the GDR regime had long since gone to bed. Now things that belonged together were growing together.

German chancellor Helmut Kohl and German president Richard von Weizsäcker at the Reichstag celebration of German unity immediately after its realization on October 3, 1990.

The Allies leave in 1994. Since 1945, the Americans, British and French have guaranteed West berlin's freedom. The Soviet troops march off separately. Berlin is again sovereign.

BERLIN TODAY

Berlin is a party for everybody – and the celebration began with the fall of the wall. In 1994, for example, the Allies withdrew: The Americans, British and French. Occupation law was valid to the end in Berlin. Every Monday, the mayor had to report to the US city commander – and not to drink coffee.

People are thorough-goingly working their way through the GDR past; nothing is to be swept under the rug. There is a federal authority for Stasi files and a Land commissioner whose sole occupation is dealing with questions of GDR injustices. It took longer to come to terms with the Nazi dictatorship as many wanted to block out the Nazi past. The fact that the older generation remained silent and refused to talk about the annihilation of the Jews was one of the factors in the 1968 unrest.

Citizens rights activists and members of opposition groups storm the headquarters of the state security ministry in Berlin on January 15, 1990. The files will be decisive in the work of evaluating the SED dictatorship.

The wrapping of the Reichstag building, the first big event jointly conducted by East and West Berliners. Jeanne Claude and Christo had been planning it for 23 years, the German parliament granted permission in a roll-call vote.

The first big celebration for the East and West was the wrapping of the Reichstag building by Christo. The artistic transcendence of this symbol of parliamentarism filled millions with a happy feeling of shared peace. Berlin celebrated the reconstruction of the Potsdamer Platz, a wasteland between East and West that was now given new life.

Now every committed Berliner became a city planner. How should our Berlin look now? Is it possible to allow developers to build modern high rises in the historical city center? Is the structure of the city to be dismantled in order to create a new Berlin – as was done after the war in the East and West? Or is the cityscape to be linked to our past?

The Potsdamer Plats in 1996, the biggest construction site in Europe. Divers pour the foundations because the groundwater level is just under the surface. "A new downtown is created."

The 1999 Love Parade. The event has stamped Berlin's image as a party town for ten years. A million young people celebrate on the Straße des 17. June in the Tiergarten borough.

Twenty years after the fall of the Berlin Wall, visitors come in droves – around the world, Berlin has become extremely hip. But they can no longer find anything of the Wall. A new debate has begun as to how the traces of the murderous splitting of the city could be made recognizable in the cityscape.

Young people no longer know exactly where East and West were. Wasn't the affluent, chic Prenzlauer Berg borough part of the West? And the impoverished boroughs of Neukölln and Wedding, weren't they in the East?

And many people in the East are aggrieved by a lack of recognition of the lives they lived in the GDR.

Berlin is continually becoming, never

The 2006 World Soccer Championship in Berlin. Germany came in third, only Italy and France squeezed in front. We celebrate all the same, a party for everybody, we really know how live it up in Berlin.

2007. The East German Palace of the Republic is torn down. After a long public debate, the German parliament decided by a two-thirds majority to rebuild the city castle for public uses.

being. Never finished, always dynamic, fast, and looking to change. This is one of the threads that runs through her history. The other one is tolerance. As Frederick the Great said: "Here, everyone is to be happy in his own way." With reference to religion: "And if the Turks come, we'll build mosques for them." Now both the Turks and the mosques are here. The Turkish middle class is performance-oriented. There are problems integrating Arab and Turkish families that cannot keep up and in which academic achievement is a low priority. Would Friedrich have pressured them? In any case, his mentality continues today: tolerance is a dominant characteristic in the city. The mayor is openly gay; former East Berlin communists sit in the Abgeordnetenhaus, the Berlin parliament, under new names, and are even members of the government. It is easy to live in Berlin,

and not expensive, compared to other metropolises. That is why so many young people from everywhere in the world are again coming to Berlin. The love of freedom is just as important to them as to the native-born. They bring drive and the desire to accomplish something in Berlin. Everybody gets his opportunity here. With or without the time to draw a breath.

The castle will be rebuilt, with its dome. It was a Berlin landmark for 500 years. With this mockup painted on plastic sheets, the Castle Union was able to persuade politicians and citizens in 1994-95.

TIMELINE

- 1237 First documentary mention of Cölln
- 1244 First documentary mention of Berlin
- 1443-1451 construction of the first city castle
- Friedrich Wilhelm elector of Brandenburg 1620-1688
- 1618-1648 The Thirty Years War
- Friedrich III./I. Elector of Brandenburg, King in Prussia 1657-1713, Duke 1688-1701, King 1701-1713
- Friedrich Wilhelm I. King in Prussia 1688-1740 reigned 1713-1740
- Friedrich II. King of Prussia, called "the Great" 1712-1786 reigned 1740-1786
- 1756 to 1763: The Seven Years War (French and Indian War in the American theater of operations)
- Friedrich Wilhelm II. King of Prussia 1744-1797 reigned 1786-1797
- Friedrich Wilhelm III. King of Prussia 1770-1840 reigned 1797-1840
- 1806 The French occupation of Berlin begins with Napoleon's march through the Brandenburg Gate (until December 1808)
- Friedrich Wilhelm IV. King of Prussia 1795-1861 reigned 1840-1858, following a stroke, the king's brother, Wilhelm, served as regent
- 1848 The March revolution
- Wilhelm I. King of Prussia, German Emperor 1797-1888 prince regent from 1858, King from 1861, Emperor from 1871
- 1871 Founding of the German Empire in Versailles
- Friedrich III. King of Prussia, German Emperor 1831-1888 reigned 9 March -15 June 1888
- Wilhelm II. King of Prussia, German Emperor 1859-1941 reigned 1888-1918
- 1914-1918 First World War
- 1918-1933 Weimar Republic
- 30. January 1933 Hitler is named Chancellor
- 1939-1945 Second World War
- 1945 Division of Berlin into four sectors
- 24 June 1948 bis 12 May 1949 Berlin Blockade
- 1949-1989 German Democratic Republic
- 13 August 1961 Construction of the Berlin Wall
- 9 November 1989 Fall of the Berlin Wall
- 1994 Withdrawal of the WW II Allies from Berlin
- 2006 World Soccer Championship in Berlin
- 2010 200th anniversary of the Humboldt University

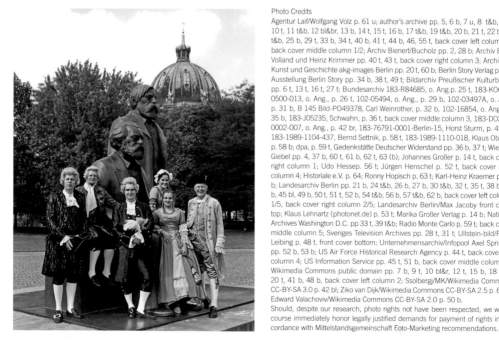

Historiale, the history festival. Collaborators of Berlin Story and Historiale stand in front of Marx and Engels, bringing the time of Friedrich the Great, the 18th century, to life in 2008.